Where is Number 11?

Written by **Keisha Juanita**
Illustrated by **Michael Angelo Go**

MVJ, I love you and the way you see the world.

Where is NUMBER 11? Is 11 in the trees?

Do you see it on those knees?

Is 11 mixed with veggies?

Is 11 shinning down from the sky?

WHERE IS NUMBER 11?

Do you see it on the door?

Is 11 on the floor?

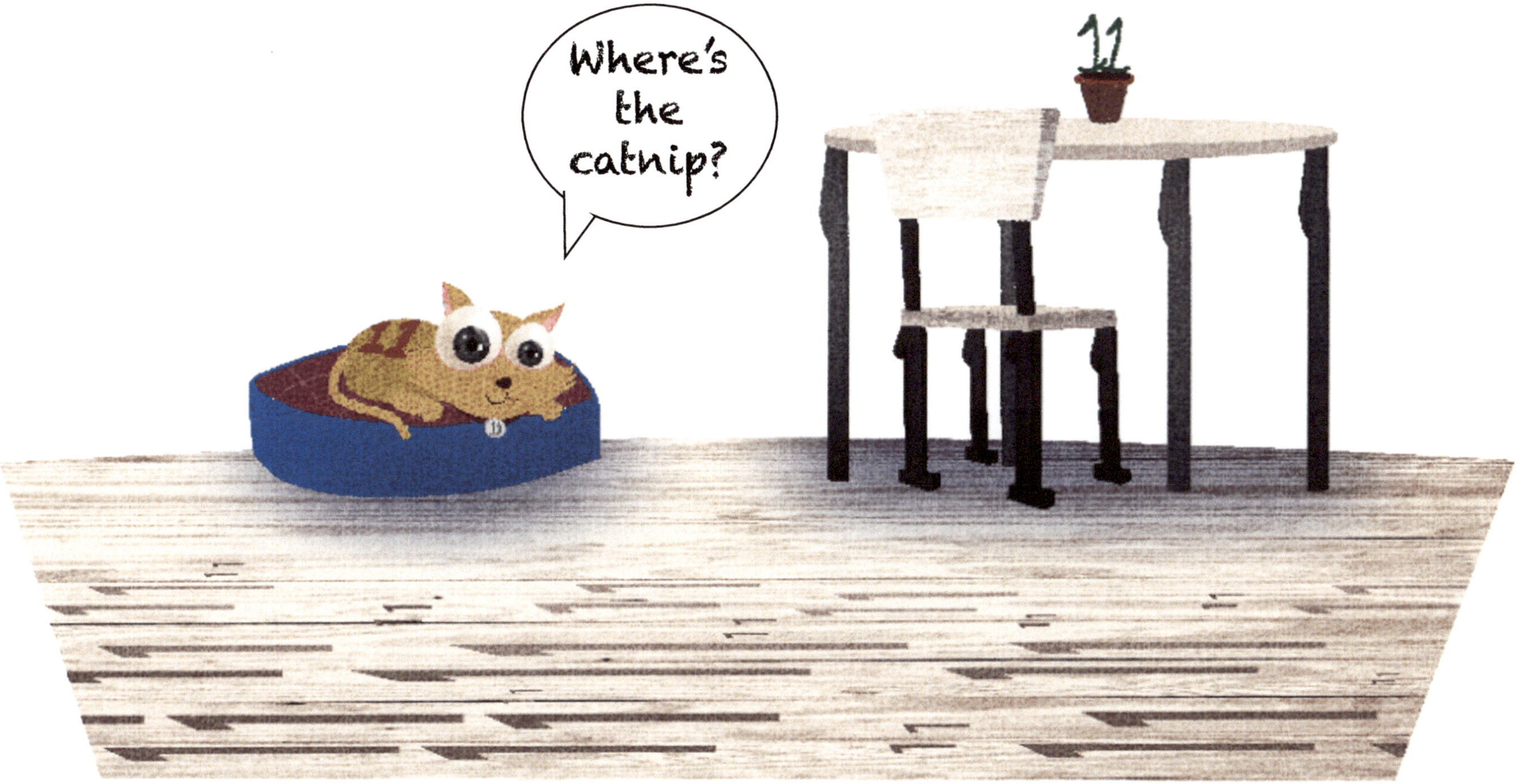
Where's the catnip?

Look, the number's on your hand!

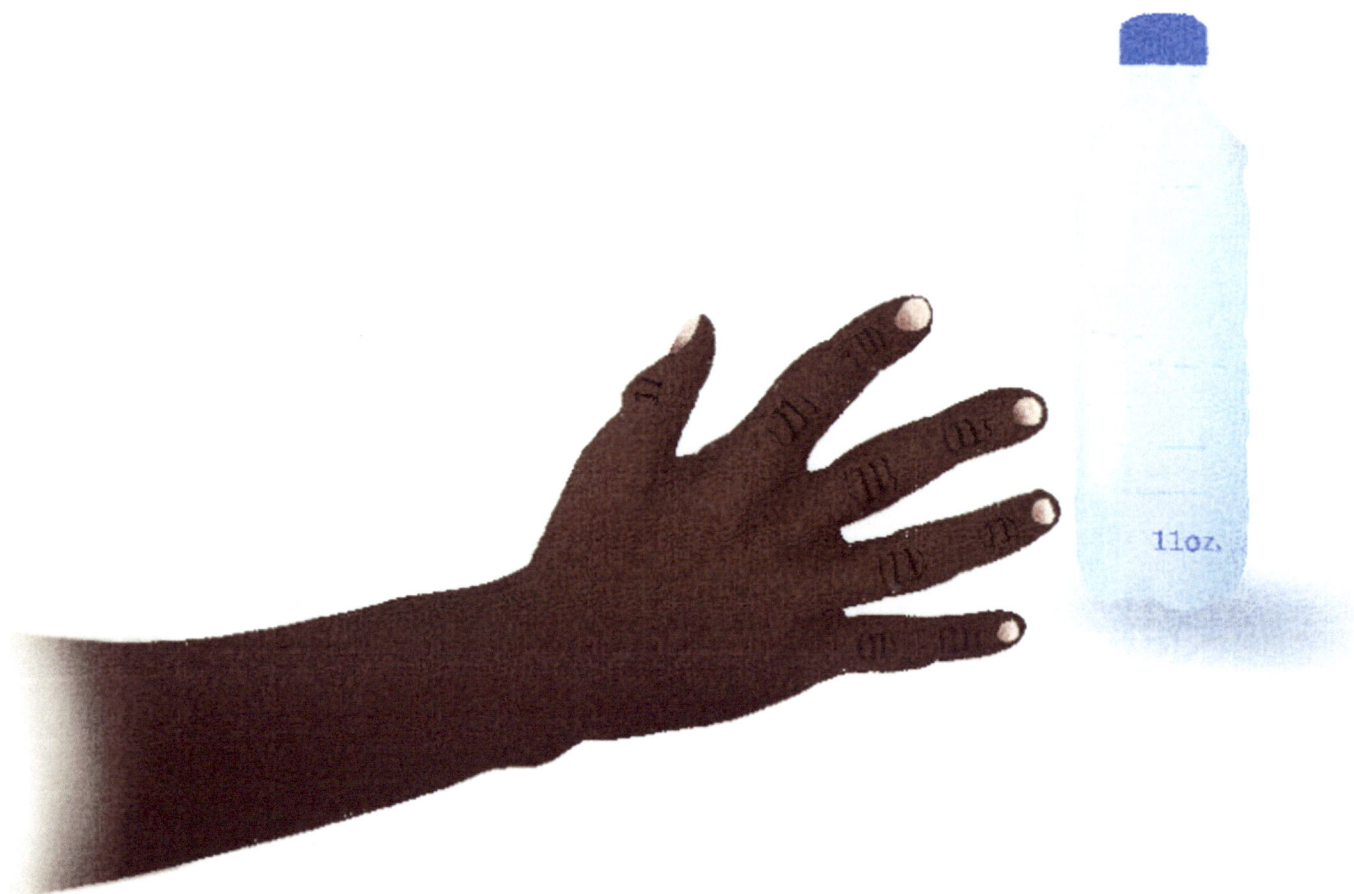

11oz.

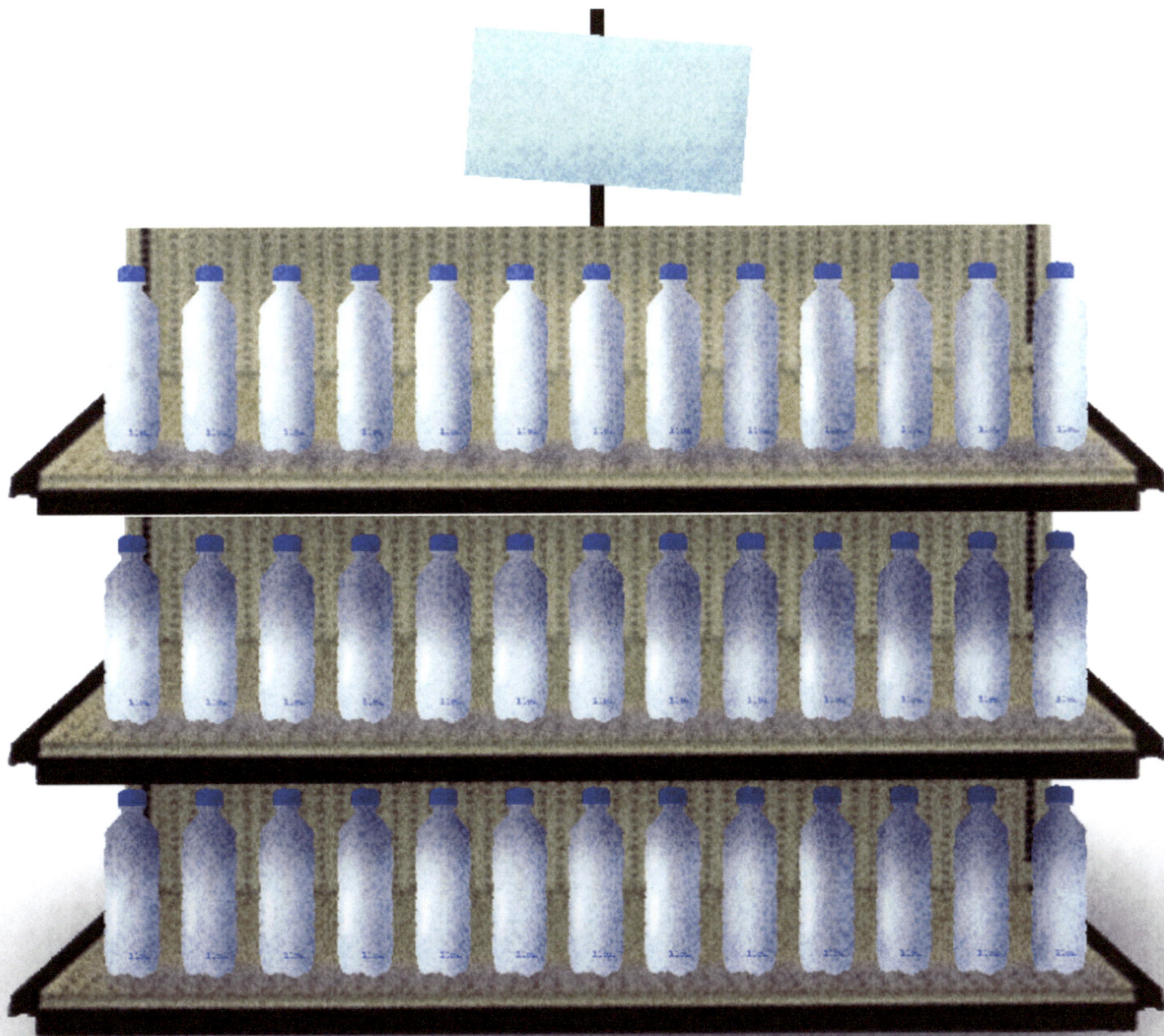

Is 11 in the sand?

WHERE IS NUMBER 11?

11 can be on all things...

Does 11 look like green beans?

Is it on that zebra's back?

Are you hungry?

Where's 11 on these snacks?

11 can be anywhere.
All you need to do is stare!

Take a look over here! 11 can be on these toads or on cars that drive a winding road.

11 is right on the clock!

It doesn't have to rhyme or rock!

11 comes after the number 10.

So take a look around and then...

When you go out to explore, you'll find yourself looking for more!

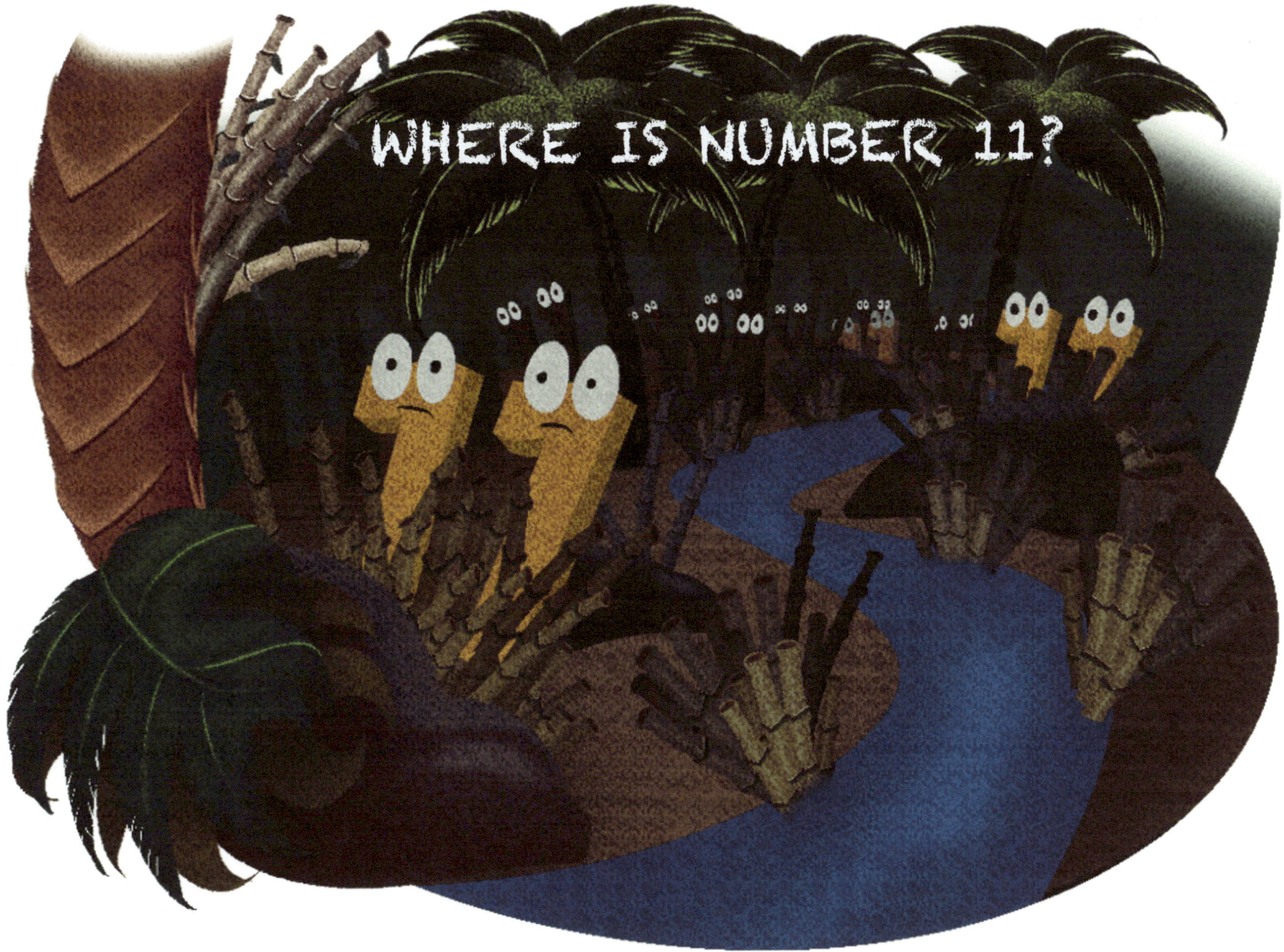

WHERE IS NUMBER 11?

FUN TRIVIA QUESTIONS

1. Which snacks look like 11's?

2. How many green beans are featured?

3. How many 11's beam down from the sun?

4. How many animals did you see throughout the book?

5. Which page is your favorite and why?

About the Author

Keisha Juanita is an American author and full-time HR professional from Prince George's County, Maryland. Keisha is passionate about writing. During the decline of the Coronavirus pandemic, she published her first children's book, Grandma's Love.

She is an active mother to a child on the autism spectrum. She has partnered with organizations, such as The One World Center for Autism, as a former Board Member to promote awareness about autism support services, participate in community outreach initiatives, and by volunteering her time to provide respite services to caregivers. Additionally, Keisha served as a Court Appointed Special Advocate (CASA) within PG County to support abused and neglected children.

Keisha's son possesses an intense fascination with letters, numbers, languages, and geography. Inspired by her son and determined to see him thrive, she used her ingenuity and creativity to propel the development of his natural STEM gifts by writing and designing this book. Keisha hopes that others who possess an intense love of numbers will also find joy in, Where is Number 11?

Keisha received her BA in Communications and MS in Marketing from the University of Maryland.

For more information about Keisha Juanita or to find her other published works, please visit, www.keishajuanitabooks.com.

www.ingramcontent.com/pod-product-compliance
Lightning Source LLC
Chambersburg PA
CBHW042107090426

42811CB00018B/1877